WEALTH MASTERY:THE ULTIMATE GUIDE TO MAKING MONEY AND BUILDING FINANCIAL FREEDOM.

TABLE OF CONTENTS:

CHAPTER 1
1. Introduction
- Welcome to Wealth Mastery
- Why Financial Freedom Matters
- Setting Your Money Mindset for Success

CHAPTER 2
2. Understanding the Basics of Money
- The Psychology of Money
- Differentiating Assets and Liabilities
- Budgeting and Saving Strategies

CHAPTER 3
3. Generating Income Streams
- Exploring Traditional Employment Opportunities
- Freelancing and Gig Economy
- Building Passive Income Streams

CHAPTER 4
4. Investing Wisely
- Introduction to Investing
- Stocks, Bonds, and Mutual Funds
- Real Estate Investments
- Cryptocurrency and Alternative Investments

CHAPTER 5
5. Entrepreneurship and Business Ventures
- Identifying Business Opportunities
- Business Planning and Execution
- Scaling Your Business for Growth

CHAPTER 6

6. Harnessing the Power of Technology
   - Leveraging Online Platforms and Tools
   - E-commerce and Dropshipping
   - Affiliate Marketing and Digital Products

CHAPTER 7
7. Financial Planning and Wealth Management
   - Creating a Personal Financial Plan
   - Strategies for Wealth Preservation
   - Estate Planning and Retirement

CHAPTER 8
8. Overcoming Challenges and Pitfalls
   - Common Money Mistakes to Avoid
   - Dealing with Debt and Financial Setbacks
   - Staying Motivated on Your Financial Journey

CHAPTER 9
9. Achieving Financial Freedom
   - Defining Your Financial Goals
   - Creating Multiple Streams of Income
   - Building Long-Term Wealth and Legacy.

GENRE: Personal Finance, Wealth Building, Entrepreneurship

DESCRIPTION:
"Wealth Mastery" is your comprehensive guide to mastering the art of making money and achieving financial freedom. Whether you're a beginner just starting your financial journey or a seasoned investor looking to diversify your portfolio, this ebook provides practical strategies, actionable tips, and valuable insights to help you build wealth and secure your financial future. From understanding the basics of money management to exploring various income-generating opportunities, investing wisely, and navigating the world of entrepreneurship, this ebook covers everything you need to know to take control of your finances and build lasting wealth.

CHAPTER 1: **INTRODUCTION:

Welcome to "Wealth Mastery," where we embark on a journey to unlock the secrets of making money and building financial freedom. In today's dynamic world, mastering your finances is not just a luxury; it's a necessity. Whether your goal is to live a life of abundance, retire early, or leave a legacy for future generations, this ebook will equip you with the knowledge, tools, and strategies you need to turn your financial dreams into reality.

2. Why Financial Freedom Matters:
Financial freedom isn't just about having an abundance of money; it's about having the freedom to live life on your own terms. Achieving financial freedom provides you with the ability to pursue your passions, spend time with loved ones, and contribute meaningfully to causes that matter to you. Moreover, financial freedom offers peace of mind, security, and the opportunity to create a legacy that extends beyond your lifetime. By understanding the significance of financial freedom, you can harness the motivation and determination needed to embark on the journey towards wealth mastery.

3. Setting Your Money Mindset for Success:
Your mindset plays a crucial role in determining your financial success. By cultivating a positive and proactive money mindset, you can overcome limiting beliefs, develop healthy financial habits, and cultivate a mindset of abundance. In this section, we will explore practical strategies for reframing your thoughts about money, embracing a growth mindset, and aligning your beliefs with your financial goals. With the right mindset, you can overcome obstacles, seize opportunities, and unlock your full potential on the path to wealth mastery.

CHAPTER 2: UNDERSTANDING THE BASICS OF MONEY

1. The Psychology of Money:
Understanding the psychology of money is essential for achieving financial success. Our attitudes, beliefs, and behaviors surrounding money influence our financial decisions and outcomes. In this section, we delve into topics such as money mindset, emotional spending, and the impact of societal influences on our financial behavior. By gaining insights into our relationship with money, we can cultivate a healthier mindset, make more informed decisions, and ultimately, take control of our financial destiny.

2. Differentiating Assets and Liabilities:
Differentiating between assets and liabilities is fundamental to building wealth. Assets are resources that generate income or appreciate in value over time, while liabilities are expenses or debts that drain your resources. In this section, we explore various types of assets, including real estate, stocks, and business investments, and discuss how to leverage them to grow your wealth. By understanding the difference between assets and liabilities, you can make strategic financial decisions that propel you towards financial freedom.

3. Budgeting and Saving Strategies:
Budgeting and saving are the foundation of financial stability and success. In this section, we provide practical tips and strategies for creating a budget that aligns with your financial goals, tracking your expenses, and maximizing your savings potential. We also discuss the importance of emergency funds, retirement savings, and automated savings plans in building a solid financial foundation. By implementing effective budgeting and saving strategies, you can achieve greater financial security, resilience, and peace of mind.

CHAPTER 3: GENERATING INCOME STREAMS

1. Exploring Traditional Employment Opportunities:
Traditional employment opportunities provide a stable source of income and often come with benefits such as health insurance, retirement plans, and paid time off. In this section, we explore various avenues for traditional employment, including full-time positions, part-time jobs, and contract work. We discuss strategies for finding job opportunities, crafting compelling resumes and cover letters, and acing job interviews. Additionally, we delve into the importance of networking, professional development, and advancing your career within traditional employment settings.

2. Freelancing and Gig Economy:
The rise of the gig economy has revolutionized the way people work, offering flexibility, autonomy, and diverse income opportunities. In this section, we delve into the world of freelancing and gig work, exploring platforms such as Upwork, Fiverr, and TaskRabbit that connect freelancers with clients in need of services. We discuss how to identify your skills and expertise, create a standout freelance profile, and effectively market your services to attract clients. Additionally, we explore the pros and cons of freelancing, managing client relationships, and maximizing your earning potential in the gig economy.

3. Building Passive Income Streams:
Passive income streams offer the opportunity to earn money with minimal ongoing effort or time investment. In this section, we explore various passive income opportunities, including rental properties, dividend-paying stocks, royalties from creative works, and affiliate marketing. We discuss the benefits of passive income, such as financial freedom, flexibility, and the potential for wealth accumulation over time. Additionally, we provide practical tips and strategies for building and diversifying your passive income streams, as well as considerations for managing and optimizing your passive income sources for long-term success.

CHAPTER 4: INVESTING WISELY

1. Introduction to Investing:
Investing is the process of allocating resources, such as money or time, with the expectation of generating a positive return in the future. In this section, we introduce the fundamentals of investing, including the importance of setting investment goals, understanding risk and return, and developing a diversified investment portfolio. We also explore different investment vehicles and strategies, as well as key principles such as compound interest and dollar-cost averaging. By gaining a solid understanding of the basics of investing, you can make informed decisions and effectively grow your wealth over time.

2. Stocks, Bonds, and Mutual Funds:
Stocks, bonds, and mutual funds are among the most common investment vehicles available to investors. In this section, we delve into each of these asset classes, discussing their characteristics, benefits, and risks. We explore how stocks represent ownership in a company and offer the potential for capital appreciation and dividends, while bonds are debt securities that provide regular interest payments and return of principal at maturity. Additionally, we discuss mutual funds, which pool money from multiple investors to invest in a diversified portfolio of stocks, bonds, or other assets. By understanding the nuances of stocks, bonds, and mutual funds, you can build a well-rounded investment portfolio tailored to your financial goals and risk tolerance.

3. Real Estate Investments:
Real estate investments offer the potential for long-term appreciation, rental income, and portfolio diversification. In this section, we explore various avenues for investing in real estate, including rental properties, real estate investment trusts (REITs), and real estate crowdfunding platforms. We discuss the benefits of real estate investing, such as tax advantages, inflation hedging, and potential for passive income. Additionally, we provide practical tips and considerations for evaluating real estate opportunities, financing investment properties, and managing rental properties effectively. By incorporating real estate investments into your portfolio, you can enhance your overall investment returns and build wealth over time.

4. Cryptocurrency and Alternative Investments:
Cryptocurrency and alternative investments represent non-traditional asset classes that offer unique opportunities and risks for investors. In this section, we explore the growing popularity of cryptocurrencies such as Bitcoin, Ethereum, and Litecoin, discussing their potential as a store of value, medium of exchange, and speculative investment. We also delve into alternative investments such as precious metals, collectibles, and peer-to-peer lending platforms, exploring their role in diversifying investment portfolios and mitigating risk. Additionally, we discuss key considerations and risks associated with investing in cryptocurrency and alternative assets, as well as strategies for incorporating these investments into a well-balanced portfolio. By exploring cryptocurrency and alternative investments, you can uncover new avenues for potential growth and diversification in your investment strategy.

CHAPTER 5: ENTREPRENEURSHIP AND BUSINESS VENTURES

1. Identifying Business Opportunities:
Identifying business opportunities is the first step towards entrepreneurship and building a successful business. In this section, we explore various methods for identifying business opportunities, including market research, trend analysis, and problem-solving approaches. We discuss how to identify unmet needs or gaps in the market, assess competition, and evaluate the feasibility and potential profitability of business ideas. Additionally, we explore emerging trends, technologies, and industries that present lucrative opportunities for entrepreneurs. By honing your skills in identifying business opportunities, you can uncover promising ventures and set the stage for entrepreneurial success.

2. Business Planning and Execution:
Business planning and execution are essential for turning business ideas into reality and achieving sustainable growth. In this section, we delve into the importance of creating a comprehensive business plan, including elements such as market analysis, target audience identification, competitive analysis, and financial projections. We discuss strategies for setting clear goals, defining business objectives, and developing actionable plans to achieve them. Additionally, we explore the importance of effective execution, including resource allocation, project management, and monitoring progress towards business goals. By mastering the art of business planning and execution, you can navigate the complexities of entrepreneurship with confidence and increase your chances of business success.

3. Scaling Your Business for Growth:
Scaling your business for growth is essential for achieving long-term success and maximizing your impact in the marketplace. In this section, we explore strategies for scaling businesses, including expanding into new markets, diversifying product or service offerings, and increasing operational efficiency. We discuss the importance of building scalable systems and processes, leveraging technology and automation, and fostering a culture of innovation and continuous improvement. Additionally, we explore financing options for scaling businesses, including debt financing, equity financing, and strategic partnerships. By implementing effective scaling strategies, you can propel your business to new heights and unlock its full potential for growth and profitability.

CHAPTER 6: HARNESSING THE POWER OF TECHNOLOGY

1. Leveraging Online Platforms and Tools:
In today's digital age, leveraging online platforms and tools is essential for reaching a wider audience, streamlining operations, and maximizing efficiency. In this section, we explore various online platforms and tools available to entrepreneurs, including website builders, social media platforms, email marketing software, and project management tools. We discuss how these tools can help businesses enhance their online presence, engage with customers, and drive sales. Additionally, we provide practical tips and best practices for selecting and implementing the right online platforms and tools to support your business goals.

2. E-commerce and Dropshipping:
E-commerce and dropshipping have transformed the way businesses sell products and services, offering opportunities for entrepreneurs to start and scale online businesses with minimal upfront investment. In this section, we delve into the fundamentals of e-commerce and dropshipping, including how they work, their benefits and challenges, and key considerations for success. We discuss how to identify profitable niches, source products, set up an online store, and attract customers through effective marketing and branding strategies. Additionally, we explore the role of dropshipping in streamlining fulfillment and logistics, enabling businesses to focus on sales and customer experience. By mastering e-commerce and dropshipping, entrepreneurs can capitalize on the growing trend of online shopping and build profitable businesses in the digital marketplace.

3. Affiliate Marketing and Digital Products:
Affiliate marketing and digital products offer lucrative opportunities for monetizing online content and generating passive income. In this section, we explore how affiliate marketing works, including how to find and join affiliate programs, promote products or services, and earn commissions on sales. We discuss strategies for creating valuable content, building an engaged audience, and optimizing affiliate marketing campaigns for maximum results. Additionally, we delve into the world of digital products, such as e-books, online courses, and software tools, exploring how to create, market, and sell digital products effectively. By harnessing the power of affiliate marketing and digital products, entrepreneurs can diversify their revenue streams and unlock new sources of income in the digital economy.

CHAPTER 7: FINANCIAL PLANNING AND WEALTH MANAGEMENT

1. Creating a Personal Financial Plan:
Creating a personal financial plan is crucial for achieving your financial goals and securing your financial future. In this section, we explore the key components of a financial plan, including setting financial goals, assessing your current financial situation, creating a budget, and developing strategies for saving and investing. We discuss how to prioritize your financial goals, such as saving for emergencies, paying off debt, and investing for retirement. Additionally, we provide practical tips and tools for tracking your progress, adjusting your plan as needed, and staying disciplined in your financial journey. By creating a personalized financial plan, you can gain clarity, confidence, and control over your finances, setting the stage for long-term success and prosperity.

2. Strategies for Wealth Preservation:
Wealth preservation is essential for safeguarding your assets and maintaining your financial security over time. In this section, we explore strategies for protecting and preserving wealth, including diversification, asset allocation, and risk management. We discuss the importance of building a well-balanced investment portfolio that aligns with your financial goals, risk tolerance, and time horizon. Additionally, we explore strategies for minimizing taxes, protecting against inflation, and planning for unforeseen events such as market downturns or economic recessions. By implementing effective wealth preservation strategies, you can mitigate risks, preserve your capital, and ensure a secure financial future for yourself and your loved ones.

3. Estate Planning and Retirement:
Estate planning and retirement are critical aspects of long-term financial planning, ensuring that your assets are managed and distributed according to your wishes and that you can enjoy a comfortable retirement lifestyle. In this section, we delve into the importance of estate planning, including creating a will, establishing trusts, and designating beneficiaries for your assets. We discuss how estate planning can help minimize taxes, avoid probate, and provide for your loved ones after you're gone. Additionally, we explore retirement planning strategies, including saving in tax-advantaged retirement accounts, estimating retirement expenses, and developing a withdrawal strategy. By taking proactive steps to plan for your estate and retirement, you can enjoy peace of mind knowing that your financial affairs are in order and that you're on track to achieve your retirement goals.

CHAPTER 8: OVERCOMING CHALLENGES AND PITFALLS

1. Common Money Mistakes to Avoid:
Avoiding common money mistakes is essential for achieving financial stability and success. In this section, we explore some of the most prevalent money mistakes individuals make, such as overspending, failing to budget, neglecting to save for emergencies, and living beyond their means. We discuss the detrimental impact of these mistakes on long-term financial health and provide practical tips for avoiding them. By being mindful of common money pitfalls and practicing sound financial habits, you can avoid unnecessary financial stress and set yourself up for a brighter financial future.

2. Dealing with Debt and Financial Setbacks:
Debt and financial setbacks can pose significant challenges on the path to financial freedom. In this section, we discuss strategies for effectively managing debt, including creating a debt repayment plan, prioritizing high-interest debt, and exploring debt consolidation options. We also provide guidance on how to cope with financial setbacks, such as job loss, medical emergencies, or unexpected expenses. By taking proactive steps to address debt and navigate financial challenges, you can regain control of your finances and work towards achieving your financial goals.

3. Staying Motivated on Your Financial Journey:
Staying motivated on your financial journey is key to overcoming obstacles and staying on track towards your goals. In this section, we explore strategies for maintaining motivation and discipline, such as setting clear, achievable goals, tracking your progress, and celebrating small victories along the way. We also discuss the importance of surrounding yourself with a supportive network of friends, family, or financial advisors who can provide encouragement and accountability. Additionally, we explore techniques for staying inspired and focused, such as visualizing your goals, practicing gratitude, and reminding yourself of the benefits of financial freedom. By staying motivated and committed to your financial journey, you can overcome challenges, persevere through setbacks, and ultimately achieve the financial success you desire.

CHAPTER 9: ACHIEVING FINANCIAL FREEDOM

1. Defining Your Financial Goals:
Defining your financial goals is the first step towards achieving financial success and building a secure future. In this section, we explore the importance of setting clear and specific financial goals, such as saving for retirement, buying a home, paying off debt, or starting a business. We discuss strategies for prioritizing your goals, breaking them down into manageable steps, and establishing a timeline for achievement. Additionally, we delve into the SMART criteria for goal-setting—ensuring goals are Specific, Measurable, Achievable, Relevant, and Time-bound. By defining your financial goals, you can create a roadmap for your financial journey and stay focused on what truly matters to you.

2. Creating Multiple Streams of Income:
Creating multiple streams of income is essential for building resilience, diversifying risk, and increasing your earning potential. In this section, we explore various ways to generate additional income beyond traditional employment, such as freelancing, side hustles, rental income, dividends, royalties, and passive investments. We discuss the benefits of diversifying your income streams, including increased financial security and flexibility. Additionally, we provide practical tips for identifying and pursuing income-generating opportunities that align with your skills, interests, and goals. By creating multiple streams of income, you can increase your financial stability, accelerate wealth accumulation, and unlock new opportunities for growth and prosperity.

3. Building Long-Term Wealth and Legacy:
Building long-term wealth and legacy involves creating a financial strategy that extends beyond your lifetime, providing for future generations and leaving a lasting impact on the world. In this section, we explore strategies for building and preserving wealth over the long term, such as investing in appreciating assets, minimizing taxes, and estate planning. We discuss the importance of setting up trusts, wills, and other estate planning tools to ensure your assets are distributed according to your wishes and that your legacy endures. Additionally, we explore the role of philanthropy and charitable giving in leaving a positive legacy and making a difference in the lives of others. By building long-term wealth and legacy, you can create a lasting impact that transcends generations and leaves a meaningful legacy for future generations to inherit.

CLOSING REMARK:
As you journey through the pages of "Wealth Mastery," remember that building wealth is a marathon, not a sprint. Stay committed to your goals, stay disciplined in your actions, and never stop learning and growing. Your financial future is in your hands, and with the right mindset and strategies, you can achieve the wealth and freedom you desire.

AUTHOR'S NOTE:
I wrote "Wealth Mastery" with the sincere hope that it will empower you to take control of your finances and create the life of abundance you deserve. Thank you for embarking on this journey with me, and I wish you all the success and prosperity in your financial endeavors.

ACKNOWLEDGMENT:
I would like to sincerely express my gratitude to each and everyone that contributed in the writing of this article, for their invaluable insights and support in the creation of this ebook. Their expertise and guidance have been instrumental in bringing this project to fruition.

www.ingramcontent.com/pod-product-compliance
Lightning Source LLC
Chambersburg PA
CBHW062126220526
45471CB00010B/3904